and disappear. So he must  *as possible, other species ... made permanently secure.*

This book attempts to set out a few of the problems and to state the case for conservation. The facts concerning conservation have been researched and studied by experts throughout the world. Many of these experts—scientists, naturalists and others—have formed societies to continue their research and to arouse public concern over the present plight of Man and Nature.

Eventually, if they get support, these societies can influence not only the public but also governments. Then laws can be passed to ensure the conservation of Nature, natural beauty and resources. In that conservation will be included Man's own species, itself threatened and vulnerable.

We can play our part in conservation by supporting these societies. At the end of this book there is a list of some of them. And we can all make these rules and observe them at all times: never needlessly to pollute or destroy any part of Nature; never to exploit it selfishly; never to ignore it or to assume that we can live aloof from it; and always to realise that we know only the merest fragment about it.

Contents

Wild Life in Britain

by
JOHN LEIGH-PEMBERTON

Ladybird Books Ltd Loughborough

Mammals—in the past

By the time the Romans first came to Britain, the mammal population had already begun to decline. The Irish elk (a giant race of fallow deer) and several other species had already disappeared; so had the lynx and the huge aurochs, or giant wild cattle, although both of these continued to exist in continental Europe. The lynx still survives there, but the aurochs disappeared by 1627.

In 55 B.C., the Romans found brown bears in Britain and exported them to fight in the circuses of Rome. They also found wolves, beavers and wild boars. Red deer and roe deer were plentiful, wild cats still existed in southern England and martens inhabited the great forests which still covered most of the island. However, there were no rats and no rabbits.

Possibly the bear was the first species to be exterminated deliberately by Man, for it was, of course, a great menace to herdsmen and shepherds. On an island a species cannot be replenished easily from other territory, and by the tenth century the bear was extinct. The beaver possibly survived into the twelfth century; there are records of it occurring in Cardiganshire until then. It probably survived even longer in Scotland.

Wolves were always regarded as Man's enemies, and in Saxon times large bounties were paid for killing them. However, in spite of this they survived in Scotland and Ireland until well into the eighteenth century, although in very small numbers. The last English wolf is believed to have been killed at the beginning of the sixteenth century.

Brown Bear *(above)*
Wolf *(centre)* **Beaver** *(below)*

0 7214 0334 4

The age of hunting

It was after the Roman period that Man began to interfere seriously with Britain's mammal population. Until then the decline or prosperity of a species had been due either to variations in climate or to alteration of habitat.

However, as farming developed, and as weapons of destruction such as the longbow and crossbow became more efficient, the effects of Man's actions on other species became more marked. During Saxon times, an enormous amount of hunting took place, but after the Norman Conquest, in 1066, it was very rigidly controlled. Poaching of deer was punishable by death, and thus the first deliberate act of conservation took place.

However, mammals other than deer and wild boar were not protected, and anything which could be eaten or which offered any sort of threat to farming or stock-raising was killed. Thus the wild cat and the marten, as well as the wolf, were greatly reduced in numbers.

James I hunted the wild boar, which may have survived, at least in northern England, into the eighteenth century. Wild cattle also survived, though these were not the true aurochs – the giant wild cattle of Europe, but a smaller breed which were still to be found in very small numbers in the Welsh mountains as late as the seventeenth century. In the twelfth century, herds of them were rounded up and enclosed in various parks in northern England. Some of them – notably at Chillingham in Northumberland, survive today still in a pure-bred form and still as wild creatures.

Wild Cattle *(above)* **Wild Boar** *(below)*

The predators

From Tudor times onwards there was an increase in the pace at which our mammal population declined. This was due to the reclamation of land for farming, the draining of fenland (begun by the Romans), the growth of the human population and the increasing efficiency of methods of destruction. The introduction of firearms for shooting birds and mammals dates from about the middle of the sixteenth century. Firearms continued to be improved, and by the end of the seventeenth century they were in fairly common use. Thereafter, Man's power to dominate other species was almost unlimited.

The first mammals to suffer from these developments were the predators. Any mammal or bird which could kill other game, poultry or farm stock was ruthlessly destroyed. Thus, the wolf disappeared and the wild cat was driven to the most inaccessible habitats.

In the nineteenth century the preservation of game-birds for private shooting increased considerably. Game-keepers were employed to destroy the predators, and the population of badgers, polecats, stoats and weasels therefore declined. Today the badger has made a good recovery as it is no longer persecuted to the same drastic extent, but the polecat is a rare animal and exists only where it is tolerated.

The otter survived rather well until the present day, although hunted by hounds and disliked by many fishermen. It declined when its habitat, the rivers and streams, became polluted, or building and industrial development altered part of its territory. Now in some danger, the otter would probably recover if rivers were cleaned up and if it could be given some protection.

8   **Otters**

Foxes

The predator which has survived most successfully into modern times is the fox. In Roman times, and until the eighteenth century, foxes had to compete for their food with wolves and wild cats. The supply of food was limited, as farmstock – such as lambs and poultry – was not as numerous as today, and the rabbit – introduced in the thirteenth century – did not become a common animal until the eighteenth century. When the wolves and wild cats disappeared, and rabbits became more numerous, the fox population grew rapidly.

Fox-hunting became an organised sport in the eighteenth century. Because it was a sport – a form of recreation for country people – foxes were preserved to a certain extent. By the nineteenth century fox-hunting had become even more popular, and the fox's habitat, or covert, was also protected. Consequently, copses, woodland and gorse patches were not cleared for farming, and these also provided a habitat for a great variety of birds and mammals. However, in some areas where foxes became a nuisance to farming, or where hunts did not operate, they were kept in check by trapping and shooting.

To a certain extent this situation still exists. Today, foxes flourish and perform their essential function as natural predators in those areas where they are preserved and controlled by hunts. Elsewhere they are being much more ruthlessly destroyed by shooting, gassing, poisoning and trapping to such an extent that, were it not for hunting, the fox, and the habitat preserved because of him, would perhaps disappear. Already in some parts of the country he is leaving the countryside and becoming a suburban animal.

Seals

Predators perform a vitally useful part in regulating the animal populations upon which they prey, and in destroying sick or injured animals and surplus young. The relationship between prey and predator is a very delicate one, never perfect and always changing. Under ideal conditions it works very well. It works badly only when some factor, such as Man's interference, is thoughtlessly introduced. For instance, if all predators in a wood, both mammals and birds, are destroyed in order to protect game birds, the effect is highly undesirable. The number of rabbits, voles, mice and rats increases beyond all natural balance. In the early part of the present century this happened frequently.

Seals are predators within their own environment. They feed on all kinds of fish, prawns and crabs. For this reason, and because they often damage nets, they are disliked by the fishing industry. Both British species, the common seal and the grey seal, have been persecuted for many years. The excessive slaughter of seals, often brutally carried out, has made it necessary for laws to be passed protecting the grey seal between September 1st and December 31st. Recent research indicates that with suitable conservation, seals need not be a serious menace to fishermen.

Many seal pups die of starvation, and all seals suffer from the effects of oil pollution of the sea. They are prone to epidemic diseases, and annual culling is, therefore, necessary to maintain reasonable numbers of healthy animals. This culling should only be carried out by experts who do it for conservation reasons.

Common Seal and Pup

Deer

Only two species of deer are indigenous (native) to Britain – the red deer and the much smaller roe deer. Originally forest animals, both have been affected by the gradual deforestation of Britain. The red deer has adapted to a mountain or moorland habitat, such as is found in Scotland or upon Exmoor. The roe deer has adapted less easily and, during the eighteenth and nineteenth century when many forests were cleared, its numbers were greatly reduced. There has, however, been a recent improvement in the roe deer population.

Deer have always been hunted, partly for sport and partly for meat. Fallow deer were introduced, possibly by the Romans, for these purposes. They came originally from the Mediterranean area and were at first kept in parks, but many escaped and formed a wild population. Like other deer, they were preserved by law either for the king or, later, the landowners until 1831, when an Act of Parliament was passed removing protection from all deer.

Because they are mainly nocturnal and have very acute senses, deer have managed to survive fairly well, but they will only do so if their numbers are kept within a balanced relationship with their habitat and food supply. They can do immense damage to cereal and root crops, woodlands and plantations. In some areas such as Exmoor, red deer are hunted with hounds, but in Scotland they are usually shot by stalkers. This is a much better and more humane method of control than hunting and, providing it is carried out by experts using the right type of weapon, should be perfectly acceptable to conservationists.

Red Deer *(above: hind and stag)*
Fallow Deer *(centre: buck and doe)*
Roe Deer *(below: buck and doe)*

Some small mammals

The decline in animal populations is not always brought about directly by the activities of Man. To a greater or lesser extent, of course, all mammals are affected by changes in their environment due to its destruction or pollution by Man, but other and more ancient causes still persist.

Various mammals, such as voles, are affected by periodic population explosions or declines, probably due to weather factors and the degree to which food is available. Red squirrels have always been subject to periodic fluctuations (about every seven years), and their present scarcity is probably as much due to this as the destruction of their woodland habitats. The introduction and spread of the grey squirrel, often blamed for the decline of the red squirrel, has probably meant that the latter cannot recover its numbers in areas where the grey squirrel is present, but there is little evidence that the grey squirrel actually drives the red squirrel out.

In medieval times, red squirrels were treated as vermin as they were supposed to deprive the deer of food.

Climate change has always been another cause of declines. It is believed that the modern scarcity of the once fairly common dormouse is due to the fact that our winters are becoming warmer. This causes the dormouse to wake from hibernation in midwinter and to perish from exposure or starvation. Dormice are also extensively preyed upon by foxes and crows while hibernating.

Harvest mice are declining in Britain, almost certainly due to changes in farming methods and the destruction of hedgerows. Crop spraying with pesticides also affects them as they eat both grain and insects.

Red Squirrel *(above)* **Harvest Mouse** *(below: left)* **Dormouse** *(below: right)*

Rare mammals

We have already considered some of the reasons why mammal populations decline. Once we realise how very easily and quickly a species can arrive at a point of near extinction, we also realise how urgent is the need for conservation. Under modern conditions, when suitable habitats are becoming increasingly hard to find, it is very difficult for a depleted species to re-establish itself. We could quite easily lose the otter if we continue to tolerate polluted rivers. The badger will go too, if its habitat disappears. We may even lose the fox if it is left to be treated as vermin, and is gassed or poisoned. The same applies to all species which in any way conflict with Man's interests. Unless we understand what is happening and take the right actions, we could easily leave to our descendants a world without the rich variety of life that exists even now.

Some animals which were quite abundant a hundred years ago are now rarities. Those which have become really scarce are chiefly predators, but some are rare because they have been killed for their fur or because of their threat to farming.

The beautiful pine marten was hunted almost to extinction on account of its valuable fur. Originally a tree dweller, it now lives among rocks in mountainous areas of Wales, Scotland and the Lake District. Its numbers are increasing slowly in areas controlled by the Forestry Commission, who welcome it as a predator on those species likely to damage young trees.

During the nineteenth century the polecat was quite a common animal, but it was shot and trapped because of its tendency to kill poultry, game birds and almost everything else, including rodents, snakes and toads. It is now increasing in those areas where it is unmolested.

Pine Marten *(above)* **Polecat** *(below)*

Mammal pests

Some mammals in Britain have increased in numbers to the point where they have become pests. This has usually happened because no suitable predator exists in sufficient numbers to control them, and because they are naturally 'successful' and adaptable animals. On the whole, Man has not been very good at controlling them, and their increase is detrimental to other species as well as to Man himself.

The principal mammal pests in Britain are the brown rat, the rabbit, the grey squirrel, the house mouse and the black rat. Between them they do an enormous amount of damage every year, costing many millions of pounds. It is noteworthy that each one of them has been introduced into this country from abroad, either accidentally or deliberately.

The black rat was introduced to this country in the Middle Ages, probably in ships returning from the Crusades. It increased in number and spread rapidly, carrying with it the fleas which harbour the virus of bubonic plague. It has been largely replaced by the brown rat which arrived, also by ship, in the eighteenth century, carrying with it the food-poisoning organisms known as salmonella. It would be good conservation, beneficial to all other wild life, to exterminate both species completely.

Before 1953, when ninety per cent of rabbits were destroyed by disease (myxamatosis), they had caused damage to crops totalling about fifty million pounds a year. Originally introduced by the Normans, rabbits provided food and fur for many centuries, and only became pests when the controlling predators were reduced. This attractive animal is a useful source of food to predators, but humane control is absolutely essential, although complete extermination might be undesirable.

Rabbit *(above)* **Brown Rat** *(below)*

Birds—in the past

Just as there was a wide variety of mammals in Britain at the time of the Roman occupation, there must also have been many birds which no longer breed here. Records from Roman and Saxon times mention birds which today are no more than rare vagrants to Britain. At least one, the great auk, is now extinct. Others probably breeding here at that time included the crane, griffon vulture, spoonbill, eagle owl, Dalmatian pelican and gyr falcon.

Climatic changes over the succeeding centuries may have accounted for the loss of some of these birds, but others must have gone because of the loss of their habitat. The clearing of forests, the draining of fens, and the ploughing and enclosing of uplands became major threats to the bird populations. Birds were netted, trapped, shot with the bow or hunted with hawks. However, it was the improvement of the sporting gun in the seventeenth century which had the greatest impact on bird life.

Surprisingly, some birds were protected by an Act of 1534. This applied to the nesting period and included the crane, spoonbill, bittern and heron, and their eggs. The kite also received protection because of its value as a scavenger in city streets.

Protection extended to the great bustard, first mentioned as being resident here in 1460. This huge bird, the largest in Europe, was probably introduced as a table bird, or it may have arrived of its own accord from the Continent. However, because of alteration to its habitat and through persecution, it lasted here only until 1845, the last eggs having been laid in Norfolk in 1838. An attempt to re-introduce it to Britain was begun in 1970.

A Great Bustard

Game birds

British game birds have been preserved for some considerable time, and their numbers reinforced by introductions from abroad. The effect of this has been much more widespread than is generally realised.

Large areas of splendid woodland remain today only because they provide 'coverts' for pheasants. These woodlands also provide a habitat for many other birds and mammals. For the last two hundred years, game-keepers have been employed to rear and protect pheasants and, as part of their job, they have deliberately destroyed such predators as hawks, crows, stoats and foxes. This has led to an inevitable increase in the numbers of pest species such as rabbits, rats and voles upon which the predators had fed. Today, as pheasant shooting becomes increasingly expensive, the destruction of predators by game-keepers is likely to increase.

Pheasants were first introduced, as domestic birds, by the Romans. Other races have been added since, and many birds are now reared in pens. If this were not done, and if shooting ceased, the pheasant and the pheasant coverts would very soon disappear.

The partridge, a native bird, has been badly affected by modern farming activities such as the burning of stubble, destruction of hedgerows and the use of insecticides which destroy the insect food of the young birds and poison the grain upon which the adults feed.

The black grouse is another native bird whose range is shrinking. One hundred and fifty years ago it could be found in nearly every English county, but it now exists only in northern England, Wales, Scotland and on Exmoor.

Pheasant *(top)* **Black Grouse** *(centre)*
Partridge *(bottom)*

Birds of prey

Birds of prey – eagles, hawks, harriers and owls – are among the most beautiful and interesting birds to be found in Britain. Their prey consists of other forms of animal life, from insects to hares and lambs, and includes many creatures which are pests, such as rats and pigeons. Unfortunately, these birds also prey upon game birds and their chicks, and so many thousands have been killed by game-keepers.

They have been persecuted because of their predatory nature, and because of it they have also been captured and trained for falconry. Some species, such as the harrier, white-tailed eagle and goshawk, have become almost extinct in Britain. Others, such as the merlin and barn owl are becoming scarce.

Birds of prey have suffered especially from the use of chemical sprays on crops. The poison contained in the insecticides or herbicides eventually reaches the predator which has fed on a bird, mammal or insect which has eaten poisoned food. The poison accumulates in the predator's body and either forms a lethal dose or renders its eggs infertile.

Modern farming activities often result in the destruction of hedgerows – a highly important habitat for a great variety of animal life. The sparrow hawk has been particularly affected by this change; once a very common bird of prey, it is now increasingly rare.

Recently there has arisen the notion that anybody can catch, rear and train a bird of prey. Apart from the fact that it is illegal to do so, it must be emphasised that this is a wholly mistaken idea. Even in the hands of experts the training of a bird of prey is very difficult, and with amateurs almost always disastrous and often very cruel.

Sparrow Hawk *(male above, female below)*

Bird protection

Unlike most mammals, all birds – with certain exceptions – are now protected in Britain. Only authorised persons may capture or kill them or take their eggs, and other people who wish to do so for good reasons must obtain a licence for the purpose. This law was passed by Acts of Parliament in 1954 and 1967, and represents one of the great steps forward in conservation of animal life in this country.

However, it would be foolish to assume that, because of this, we can no longer harm wild birds. Often we harm them quite unwittingly. Imagine that we have found a warbler's nest; it might be that of our own native Dartford warbler, or of a migrant which has travelled all the way from Africa. If it is the latter, it has avoided being netted (as thousands are) when crossing Italy or France. It has managed to find a nesting site which has available a supply of unpolluted food and water.

Of course, we do not take the eggs, but we might go very close to the nest and possibly photograph it, taking some time over doing so. The parent bird is watching us, and if we stay too long the eggs may chill or the nest may be abandoned. At the same time a crow or magpie is also watching us. When we have gone it comes to see what we found so interesting – a nestful of eggs or nestlings! In either case, all are taken and eaten.

We must at all costs avoid this kind of disturbance, however tempting, and particularly if carried out by a group of enthusiasts. It can be just as damaging as egg-collecting; the results are the same.

Whitethroat *(top: left)*
Blackcap *(top: right)* **Dartford Warbler** *(centre)*
Reed Warbler *(bottom)*

Birdwatching

Watching birds is a much simpler activity than watching mammals. Birds are found in almost every kind of habitat; there are very many of them and most of them are diurnal (active in the day). The majority of people find them more attractive than mammals, many of which have the disadvantage of being difficult to find, secretive and primarily nocturnal. As a result, the conservation of birds in Britain has been well supported, and societies formed to promote the conservation and study of birds have been able to achieve excellent results. Very many reserves and sanctuaries now exist, areas large and small devoted to the protection of birds. Many have wardens to run them. Before visiting them it is usually necessary to apply for permits, and – of course – it must always be remembered that the sanctuary is there for the benefit of birds and not principally for birdwatchers.

Widespread interest in birds has some curious disadvantages. Too much interest by too many well-intentioned people puts too much pressure on the birds. The enthusiasm to see and photograph unusual species can drive them away from some areas and cause a species to become scarce locally. This has happened to the chough, which has forsaken many of its ancient cliff haunts and has moved to remoter areas.

The scarcer a bird is, the more desirable it becomes to illicit egg or specimen collectors and to birdwatchers and photographers, some of whom may not be over-scrupulous about how they obtain their results. The dotterel, a charming little migrant which breeds on mountain tops in Scotland, has been greatly reduced in number because it is uncommon, edible, attractive and astonishingly tame.

Chough *(above)* **Dotterel** *(below)*

Sea birds

All sea birds face dangers peculiar to their particular environment. Some sea birds, notably puffins and other members of the auk family, are declining for reasons which are entirely man-made and of recent origin.

The first and best-known danger is from oil pollution. Every year thousands of sea birds, covered with a thick coating of crude oil, are washed up on our shores. This oil has either been spilled accidentally from tankers, or has been deliberately put into the water by ships washing out their tanks at sea. The result of oil pollution is that the affected bird cannot fly, feed, swim or breathe. It floats in a water-logged condition until it dies, and is later washed ashore.

Some birds are alive when washed up. Removal of the oil is very difficult because the essential natural oil on the bird's feathers is also removed. A cleansed bird must, therefore, be kept for a long time before it can be released to the wild with any chance of survival. This is really a job for experts, and anyone wishing to help in the rescue of oiled birds should contact the nearest R.S.P.C.A. Inspector or some similar official.

Gulls, divers, grebes, auks, wildfowl, waders, petrels, shearwaters and cormorants are all possible victims. Oil pollution is not the only danger to them; poisonous chemical waste, dumped in the sea, claims many birds and the food upon which they live. Thousands of auks are shot every year off Norway, and many sea birds, trapped in fishing nets, are drowned.

Storm Petrel *(top: left)*
Kittiwake *(top: right)* **Guillemot** *(centre: left)*
Manx Shearwater *(bottom)*

Rare birds

There always have been, and always will be, birds which can be considered rare in Britain. A rare species may be the beginnings of a new population or the remnants of one which once flourished. It may be a species which can only tolerate certain conditions of climate and environment, and which can never establish itself in any great numbers.

Conservation, climate, luck, all play a part. At the present time, and in spite of some setbacks, many birds, once lost, are tending to return to us. This is largely due to a change in people's attitude towards nature. Not so long ago, any strange or unusual bird was shot – simply out of curiosity and in order to obtain a specimen. This can still happen; selfish, ignorant people still shoot the occasional honey buzzard or golden oriole. There are still people greedy enough to take the eggs of kites or ospreys, for sale to collectors. The nests of such rare birds have to be guarded night and day against vandals and egg thieves.

However, conservation has its triumphs. The snowy owl now breeds in Britain, so does the osprey, the avocet and the ruff. Golden·eagles have returned to England after two hundred years and have raised young. The black redstart has established itself and so has the black-tailed godwit. The coastal reserves harbour many rare waders.

We should perhaps decide that, if we are lucky enough to see a rare bird, we should share the knowledge only with those people whom we can trust not to disturb the bird or take its eggs.

Osprey

Bird pests

A bird can be regarded as a pest when its numbers and activities form a threat to the interests of Man or of other species. Several factors can contribute to this situation: a high breeding rate, a wide range of food items, lack of suitable predators, adaptability and wariness.

Every year birds cause millions of pounds worth of damage to crops, woodland and buildings. There has been much research into ways of preventing this damage, and limited success has been achieved.

Unlike mammal pests such as the rat, bird pests fortunately do not carry serious disease organisms, although it has been suggested that foot and mouth disease in cattle may perhaps be spread by migrant starlings.

Wood pigeons and city pigeons probably cause more damage than any other birds. City pigeons roost on and foul buildings, the cleaning of which is difficult and very expensive. Wood pigeons, with their enormous appetites, cause widespread damage to crops of every kind, and have become much bolder in recent years.

Flocks of starlings can infest a city or ruin woodland with their droppings. House sparrows cause enormous losses to grain crops, gardens and fruit. They can also infest buildings.

All these birds are 'successful' birds. They can breed throughout the year and in a wide variety of habitats, and often seem to be unaffected by the many means – shooting, poisons, traps, alarms, electric shocks – which have been devised to eliminate and discourage them. Most of the predators which would have reduced their numbers, such as the hawk and owl, have themselves been reduced by Man. The lesson is – not to destroy predators which keep down their numbers!

Starlings *(above)* **Wood Pigeon** *(below)*

Fish—salmon

The salmon is a marine fish which may be evolving gradually into a freshwater species. Most of its life is spent at sea, and it only enters rivers to breed. During the whole of its life it faces considerable hazards.

After it hatches from the egg, the salmon is known as an 'alevin', and when about five centimetres long, as a 'fingerling'. Throughout this period both egg and fish are likely to be preyed upon by other species, especially eels. When it measures from ten to twenty centimetres long, it is a 'parr' and it stays in this stage for one or two years, after which it is a 'smolt'. Smolts leave the river and take to the sea, where they spend at least two years, feeding and growing enormously and becoming full-grown salmon. During this period they are preyed upon by seals, killer whales and other predators.

Salmon return to the rivers to breed. This is a dangerous period for them, many being netted in river estuaries and others being fished for by fly-fishermen. If the river is polluted, they may succumb to poisons or to lack of oxygen. They are also prone to various epidemic diseases.

After spawning (laying about fifteen thousand eggs), salmon are exhausted, for they have not fed regularly since leaving the sea, and they return there in very poor condition. In this state they are known as 'kelts'. When they return to the sea, many go to Arctic areas such as the west coast of Greenland, where they are now netted in great numbers commercially.

On the whole, the species is considerably threatened.

Freshwater fish

Water pollution is the gravest danger to the survival of our freshwater fishes. Rivers become polluted when sewage, chemical waste products or oil enter them in excessive quantities. Also, when agricultural land is sprayed with chemical insecticides or herbicides, a large proportion of these is washed by rainfall into ditches, streams and rivers, not only causing pollution but also actually poisoning the water.

When a river is badly polluted, it no longer provides the oxygen necessary if fish, and other living things, are to exist in it. Today (1972), about one quarter of all the river water in Britain is polluted, and for some years many rivers have ceased to contain fish, insect or plant life over much of their length.

Of course, some rivers are still clean. These are often the ones which are maintained and preserved by fishing organisations, and where fish such as trout can be reared. Fishermen contribute greatly towards this form of conservation.

Elsewhere, however, thousands of fish die and, worse still, thousands are not hatched at all. It is possible, however, to re-stock a river once it has been cleaned up. This can also happen to many polluted ponds and smaller streams; recovery is possible. In 1958, the Thames was badly polluted; there were no fish at all from Richmond to Gravesend. After massive anti-pollution measures had been taken, fifty-one species were recorded in 1970 between Fulham and Southwark.

Trout *(top)* **Grayling** *(centre: above)*
Perch *(centre)* **Chub** *(centre: below)*
Dace *(bottom)*

Sea fish

Because the seas are so vast, and the number of fish in them so great, it has been easy to believe that there would always be a plentiful supply of fish for the people of the world. However, now that the human population is growing so enormously, the need for conservation of the sea, and the life in it, has become urgent. Even a thousand miles out in the Atlantic Ocean, the water is polluted in places. It is polluted at the mouth of almost every large river and near every sizeable town. In some areas it can no longer maintain life.

There are three sorts of pollution, all of which can kill fish, induce disease in them or prevent them from breeding. Pollution from oil slicks is widespread; not just from spectacular oil slicks but from the many smaller ones, the effects of which, when added together, are just as harmful.

Pollution is also caused by the greatly increased amount of sewage now being poured into the sea from expanding human populations. Pollution is also caused at sea by the dumping of dangerous chemical waste-products. Already there are parts of Britain's coast where the fish, if they survive, are not suitable for human consumption because of the chemicals they have absorbed. The sea is, in fact, dying in some places.

New threats to fish arise from overfishing, the result of increased demand and improved fishing techniques, and from the small-gauge nets used by some countries. Small-gauge nets catch fish that are too small to have reached the size at which they are capable of breeding. No two factors could deplete a species more quickly.

Haddock *(top)* **Cod** *(centre: above)*
Herring *(centre below: left)*
Pilchard *(centre below: right)* **Plaice** *(bottom)*

The sea shore

Just as other plants and animals are affected by Man's activities, so are the thousands of forms of life inhabiting the seas. In some way or other, all of them form a link in the 'chain of life', each link depending to some degree upon the others. We may not worry very much about the loss of some form of Pacific mollusc, but if its loss also means the loss of the sea otter, we mind very much. Many of our own waders and shore birds depend for their living on small crabs, shrimps and marine worms. If these minor forms of sea life are eliminated, so are the birds, fish and mammals which feed on them.

The pollution which threatens the fish must obviously affect the shell-fish, crabs, sea urchins and such things as lug worms and sea-anemones. Recently (1971) it was revealed that quite a large part of the Irish Sea, off Liverpool Bay, was so badly polluted that crabs were diseased and many forms of life formerly found there were non-existent. Industrial waste, sewage and oil pouring into the sea year after year had become too much for the tides to clear. So, part of conservation means ensuring that modern development should always be adjusted to the ability to dispose of waste products safely.

When oil slicks or oiled beaches have been treated with detergents to clear them, it has been found that the detergent is just as harmful to the minor forms of life as the oil itself. Obviously, more research into methods of treating oil slicks is urgently needed.

Shore Crab *(top)* **Common Sea Star** *(centre: left)* **Common Cockle** *(centre: right)* **Whelk** *(bottom: left)* **Sea Urchin** *(bottom: right)*

Amphibians—toads and frogs

Britain possesses eight amphibious animals. There are the three kinds of newt – the smooth, crested and palmate; two kinds of toad – common and natterjack, and three kinds of frog – common, edible and marsh. The edible and marsh frogs are 'introduced' animals which have not spread or established themselves very quickly.

Amphibians are a class of animals which evolved from fishes. Their young are hatched from eggs (spawn) laid in the water, and are at first very fish-like in appearance (tadpoles). The amphibian's life is spent partly on land and partly in the water and it feeds on a variety of insects and other food from both. Consequently it has to face dangers present both on land and in the water.

Toads and frogs are not so numerous as they were. This is possibly due to the fact that it is increasingly difficult for them to find ponds clean enough in which to deposit their spawn. It is noticeable that many ponds where once tadpoles were abundant, no longer contain them. The killing, by insecticide sprays, of insect life on agricultural land and to a certain extent in gardens, means that food for frogs and toads is more scarce. As with all animals, a shortage of food is usually followed by a reduced rate of breeding. Frogs are also being collected and used in medical research in such numbers that the species is bound to be affected.

The decline in the numbers of these animals would be a great pity, for both are good friends to the gardener and farmer.

Common Toad *(above)*
Common Frog *(below)*

Reptiles—snakes and lizards

There are only three species of lizard found in Britain. Only two of them, the common (or viviparous) lizard and the slow-worm (a legless lizard and not a snake) are at all common. The third species is the beautiful sand lizard, fast disappearing and now found in only a few localities.

Lizards like to live in dry places such as hedgerows, heaths and commons. They are often found in coastal areas and, during the present century, building growth has resulted in a reduction of the lizard population. Modern intensive agriculture does not permit rough, derelict heath or hedgerows, and thus many lizard habitats have gone; so has their food, for they feed on insects and on slugs, which pesticides destroy.

The three British snakes are the grass snake, the smooth snake and the adder. Only the last of these is poisonous and the bite, delivered only when the adder is frightened or accidentally trodden on, is very rarely fatal. In spite of this, and because most people cannot identify them, all snakes have in the past been killed on sight. The best way to conserve snakes is to leave them strictly alone and resist the temptation to keep them as pets. They are not particularly easy to feed in captivity as they prefer live foods such as frogs, lizards and even mice, though adders will sometimes eat dead food. Many of them seem to feed only at dusk.

British snakes hibernate in winter. They are preyed upon by birds such as harriers and by stoats. Loss of habitat and prey species seem to be the greatest threats to their survival.

Adder *(top)* **Grass Snake** *(centre)*
Common Lizard *(bottom)*

Insects—butterflies

Almost everything that has happened to change the British countryside during the present century has had a bad effect on butterflies. With its uncertain climate, Britain is not an ideal butterfly environment, and the draining of fenland, the ploughing of downland and the clearing of woodland and scrub have removed many suitable habitats. In the past the widespread hobby of butterfly collecting, now most undesirable, had a marked effect on the rarer species.

Until quite recently, many species of butterfly were plentiful throughout the countryside. Butterflies, their eggs and pupae have all suffered from the use of pesticides in agriculture, but the worst effects have resulted from the practice of spraying wasteland and roadsides with herbicides.

To many butterflies 'weeds' and wildflowers are essential, either as food plants or as places to lay their eggs and provide food for the caterpillars when they hatch. So the hedge brown needs brambles, the peacock needs nettles, the orange tip needs cuckoo flower, the chalkhill blue needs horsehoe vetch. Most of these 'weeds' are destroyed by herbicides or by the cultivation of the places where they grow.

The large copper butterfly became extinct in Britain in 1848, largely through the activities of collectors. In 1927 it was re-established by introduction from Holland. The food plant of the caterpillar is the great water dock, and this was specially planted at Wood Walton Fen where, protected, the butterfly now survives. This fine example of intelligent conservation suggests that other species threatened or lost to us, such as the black-veined white or the mazarine blue, might also be re-established.

Hedge Brown *(top: right)* **Peacock** *(top: left)*
Large Copper *(centre: male left, female right)*
Chalkhill Blue *(bottom left: female left, male right)*
Orange Tip *(bottom right: male above, female below)*

Glossary

Some of the words commonly used in the discussion of conservation may be unfamiliar to you. Here is a short list of some of them, with their meanings.

Covert: The name for the place where a mammal or bird lives. Usually applied particularly to foxes and pheasants.

Culling: The essential killing, for conservation purposes, of surplus, diseased animals in a colony or herd.

Deforestation: The deliberate clearing of forest, both scrub and woodland.

Diurnal: Active by day.

Ecology: The study of the relationship between all living things and their environment.

Environment: The surroundings, land, air, water in which an animal lives.

Feral: An adjective describing a species or individual animal, once domesticated, which has returned to the wild state.

Habitat: The place where an animal lives in the natural state.

Herbicide: A chemical substance made for killing vegetation.

Hibernation: A deep and prolonged winter sleep in which the pulse, breathing and heartbeat slow down and the body temperature drops below normal.

Indigenous: Native to a particular country or area.

Insecticide: A chemical substance made for killing insects.

Migrant: A foreign species which visits us to breed or spend the winter.

Nocturnal: Active at night.

Pesticide: A chemical substance made for killing pests.

Pollute: To foul, dirty, corrupt, spoil.

Vagrant: A foreign species which occurs occasionally in an area in the course of wandering or journeying elsewhere.

Viviparous: Giving birth to live young, as opposed to laying eggs.